What Are You Feeling?

FEELINGS BOOKS FOR CHILDREN

Children's Emotions & Feelings Books

BABY PROFESSOR
EDUCATION KIDS

Speedy Publishing LLC
40 E. Main St. #1156
Newark, DE 19711
www.speedypublishing.com

Copyright © 2017

All Rights reserved. No part of this book may be reproduced or used in any way or form or by any means whether electronic or mechanical, this means that you cannot record or photocopy any material ideas or tips that are provided in this book

Let's Begin With types of feelings

Happy

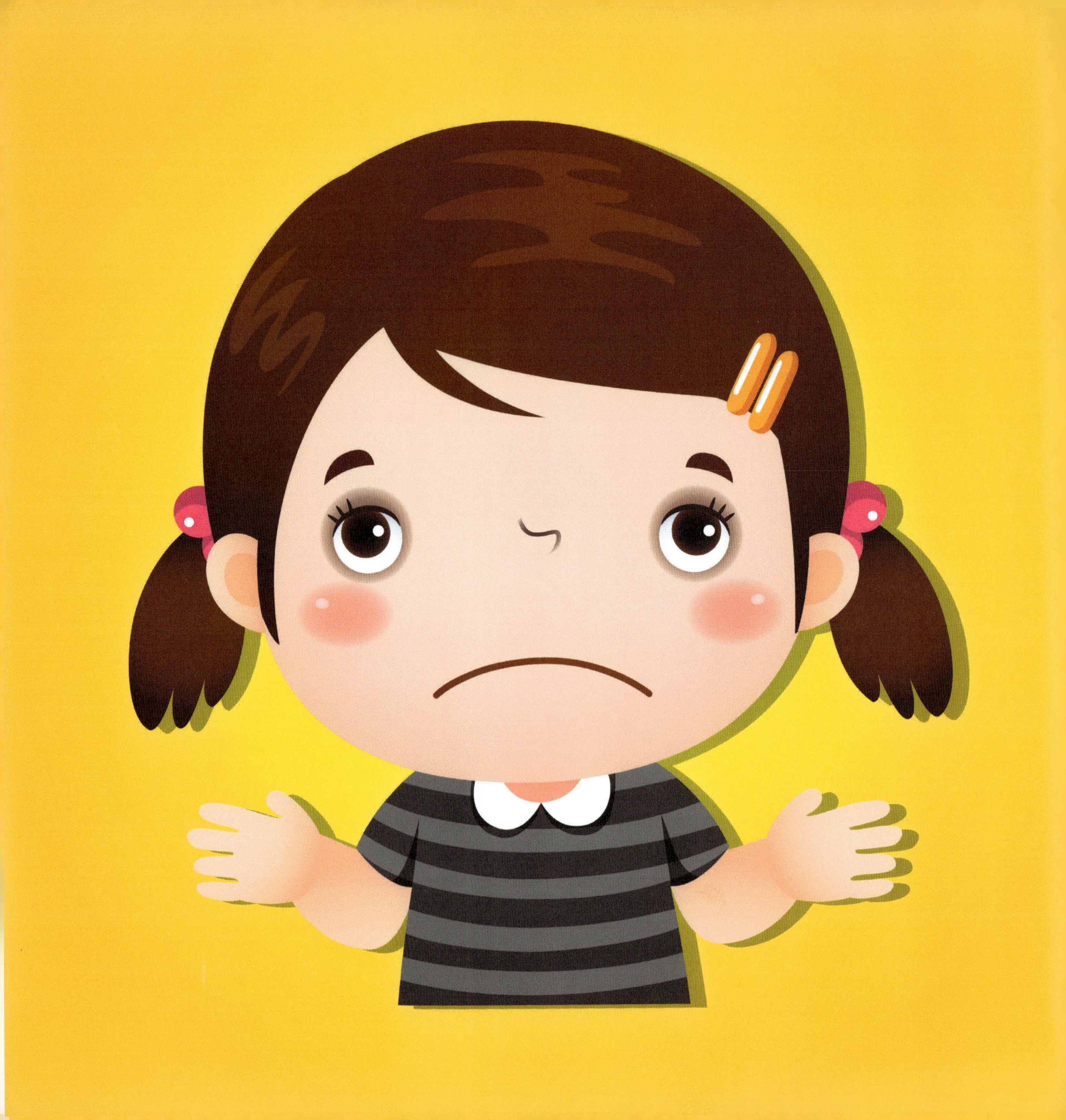

Disappointed

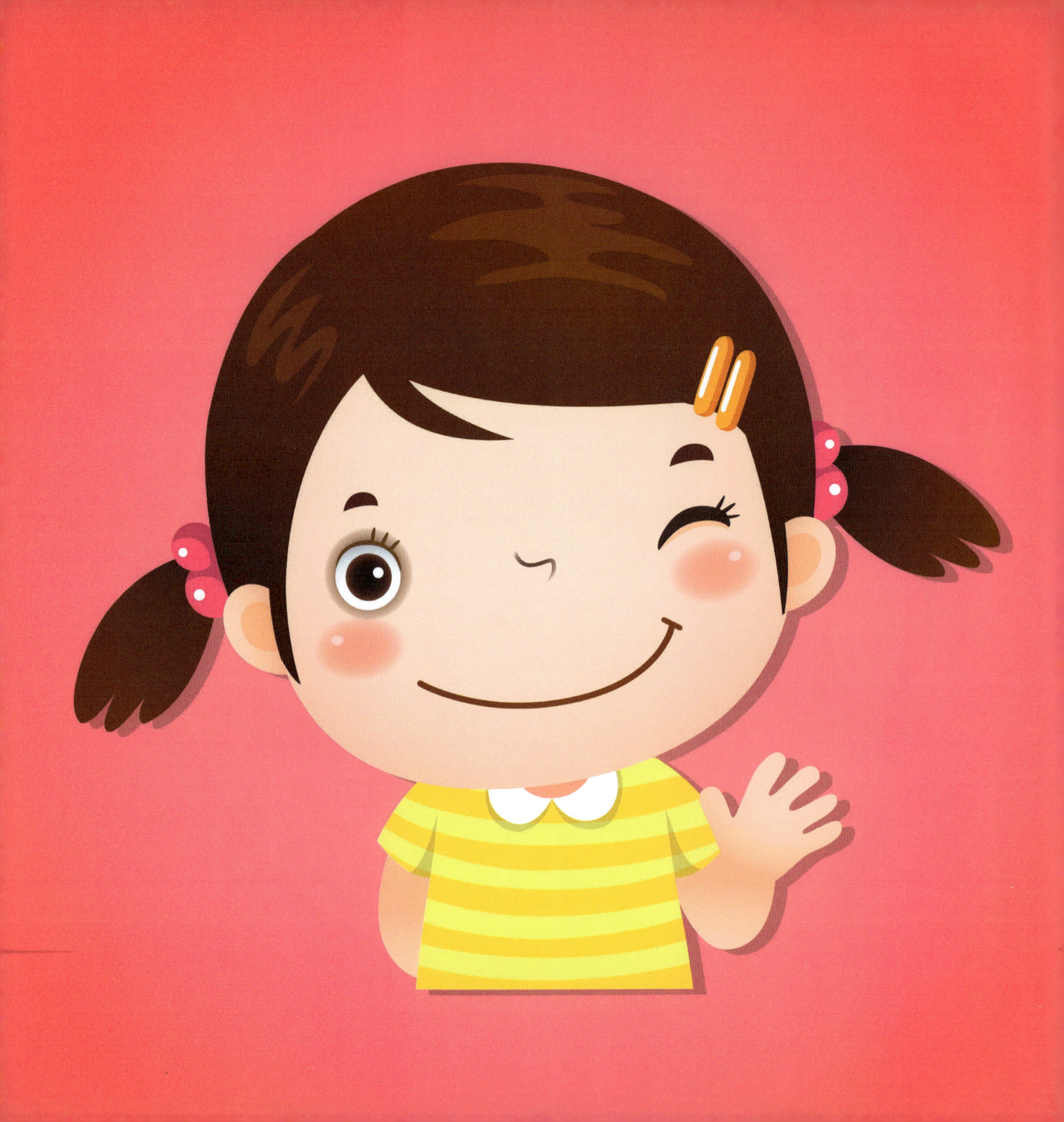

cheeky

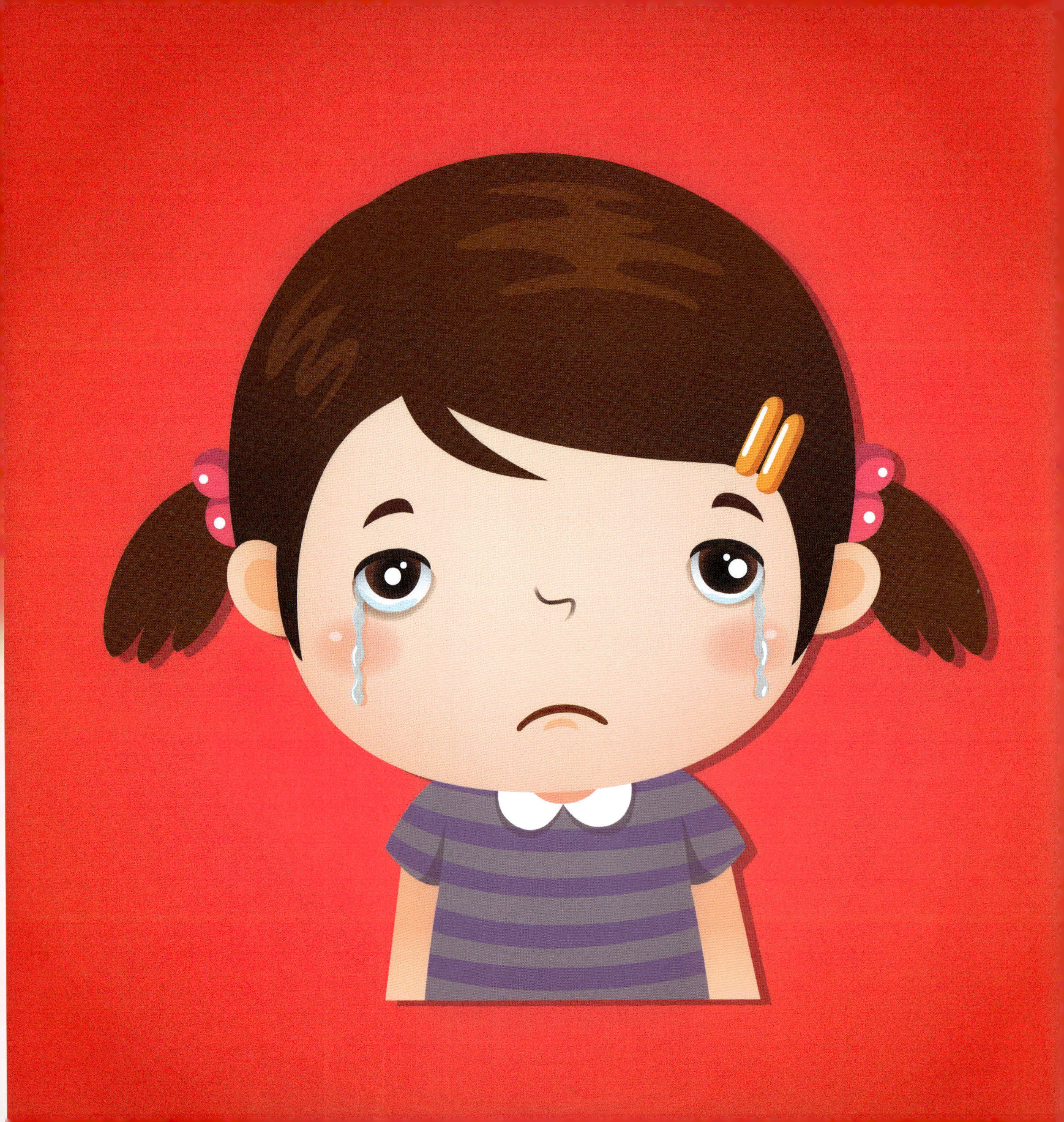

SaD

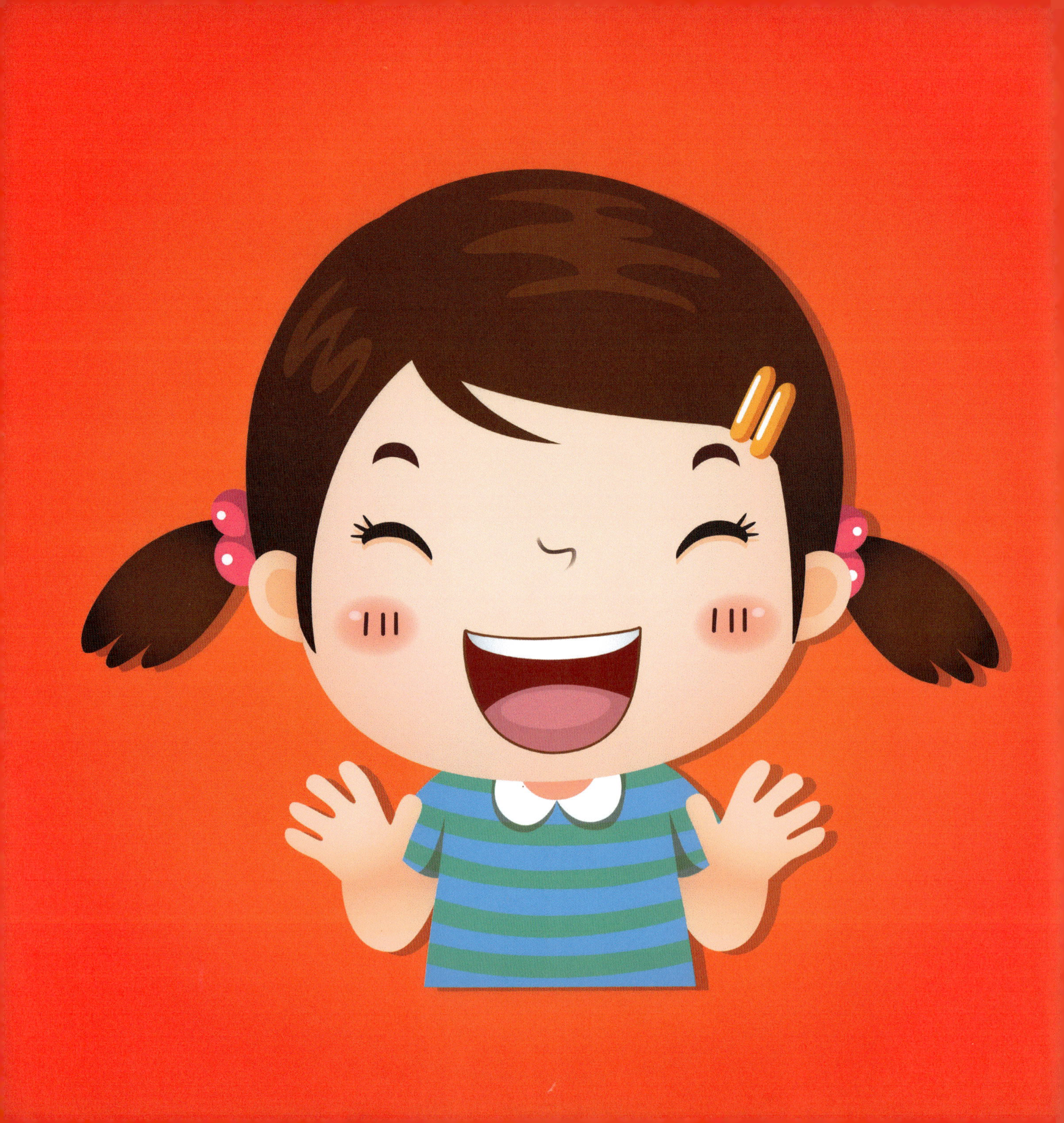

Excited

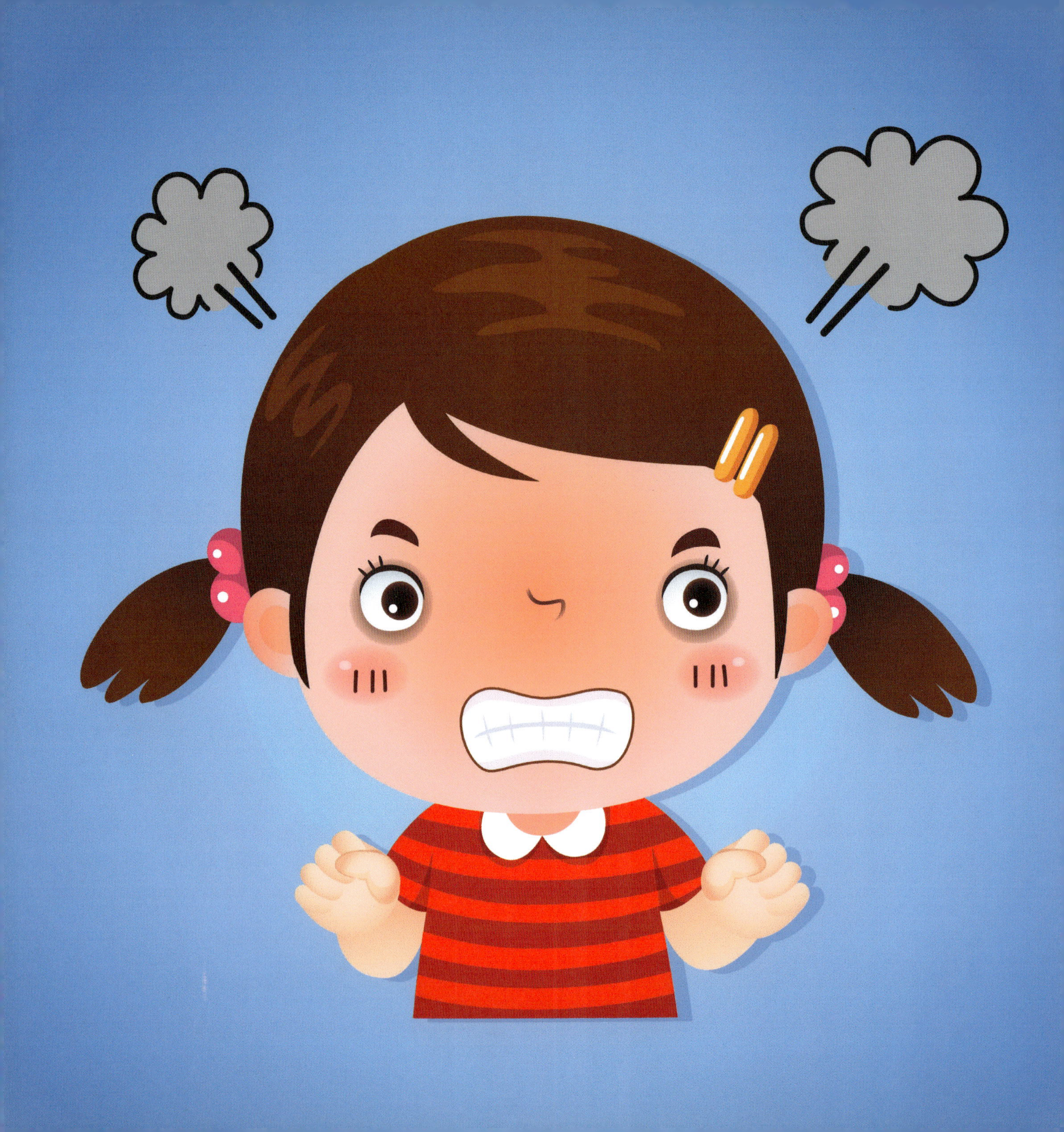

Angry

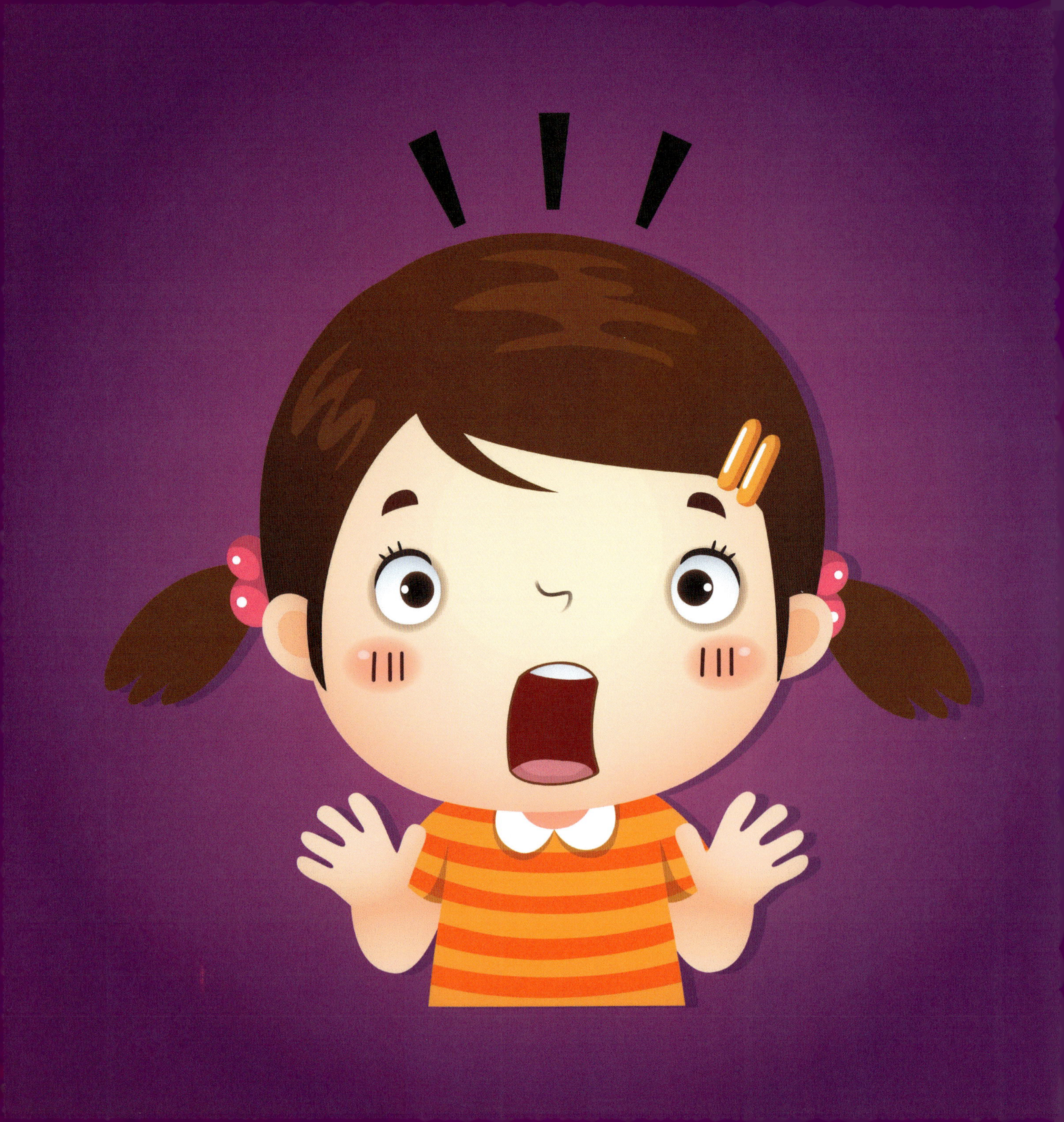

SCareD

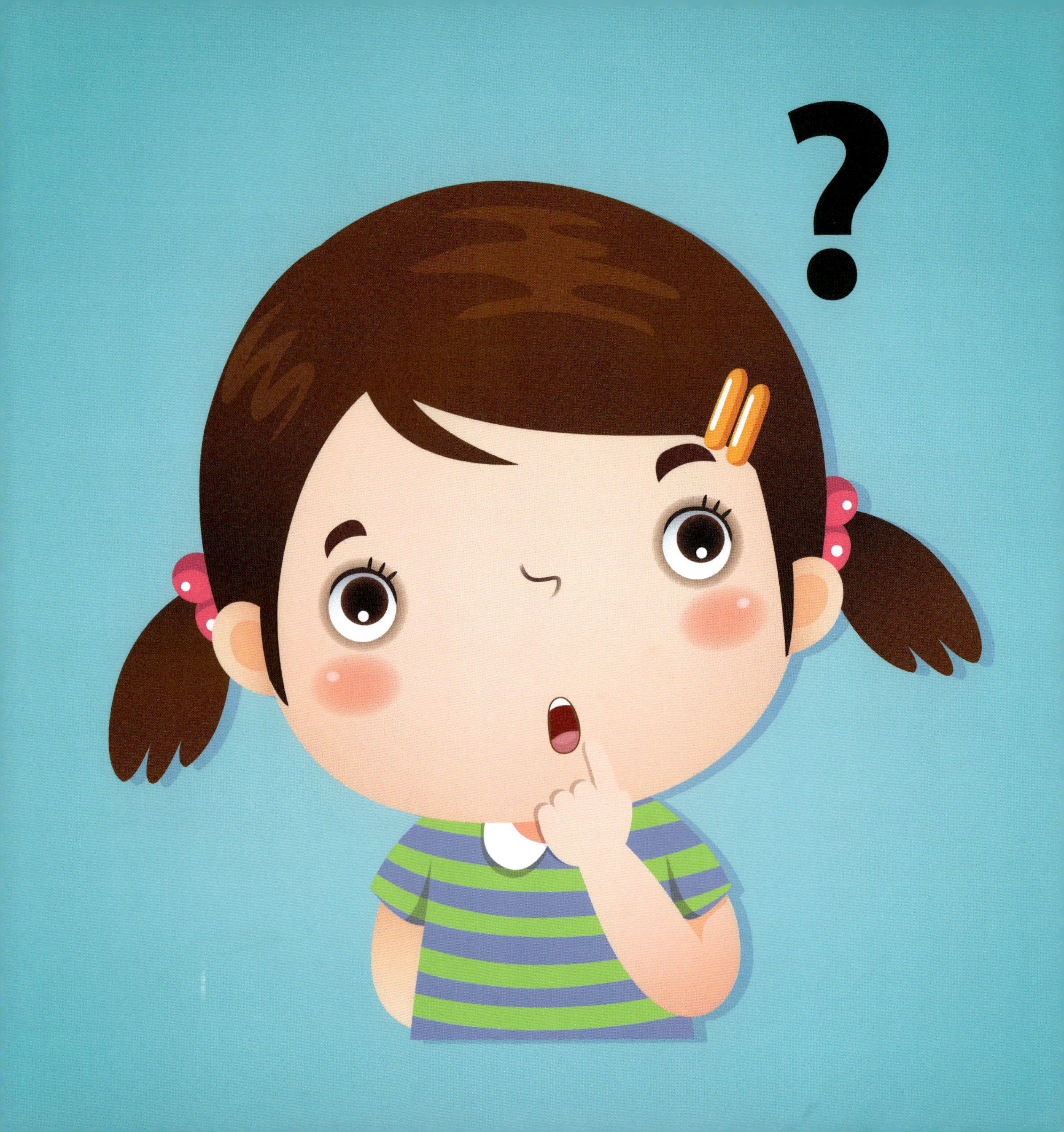

confuseD

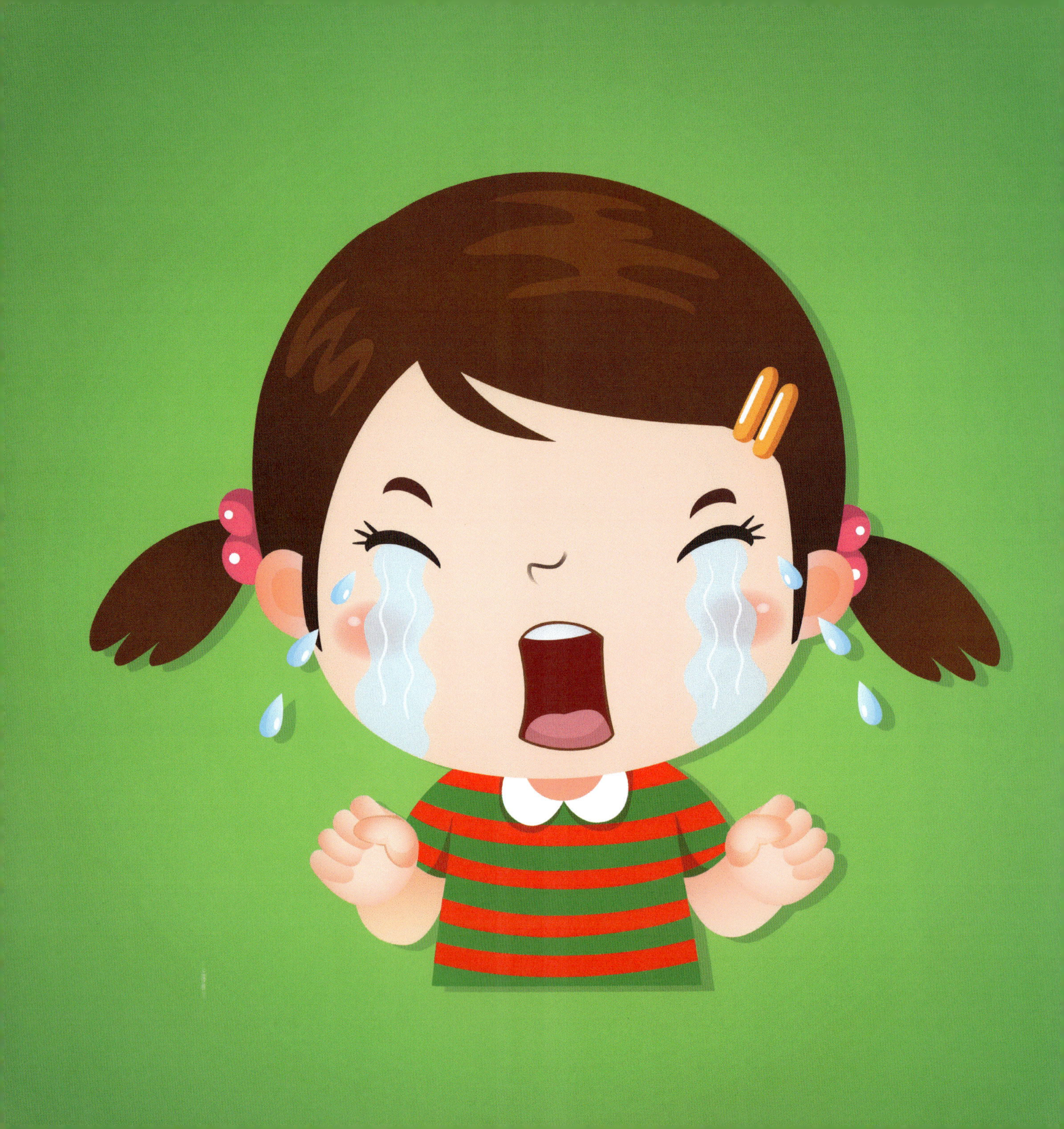

Hurt

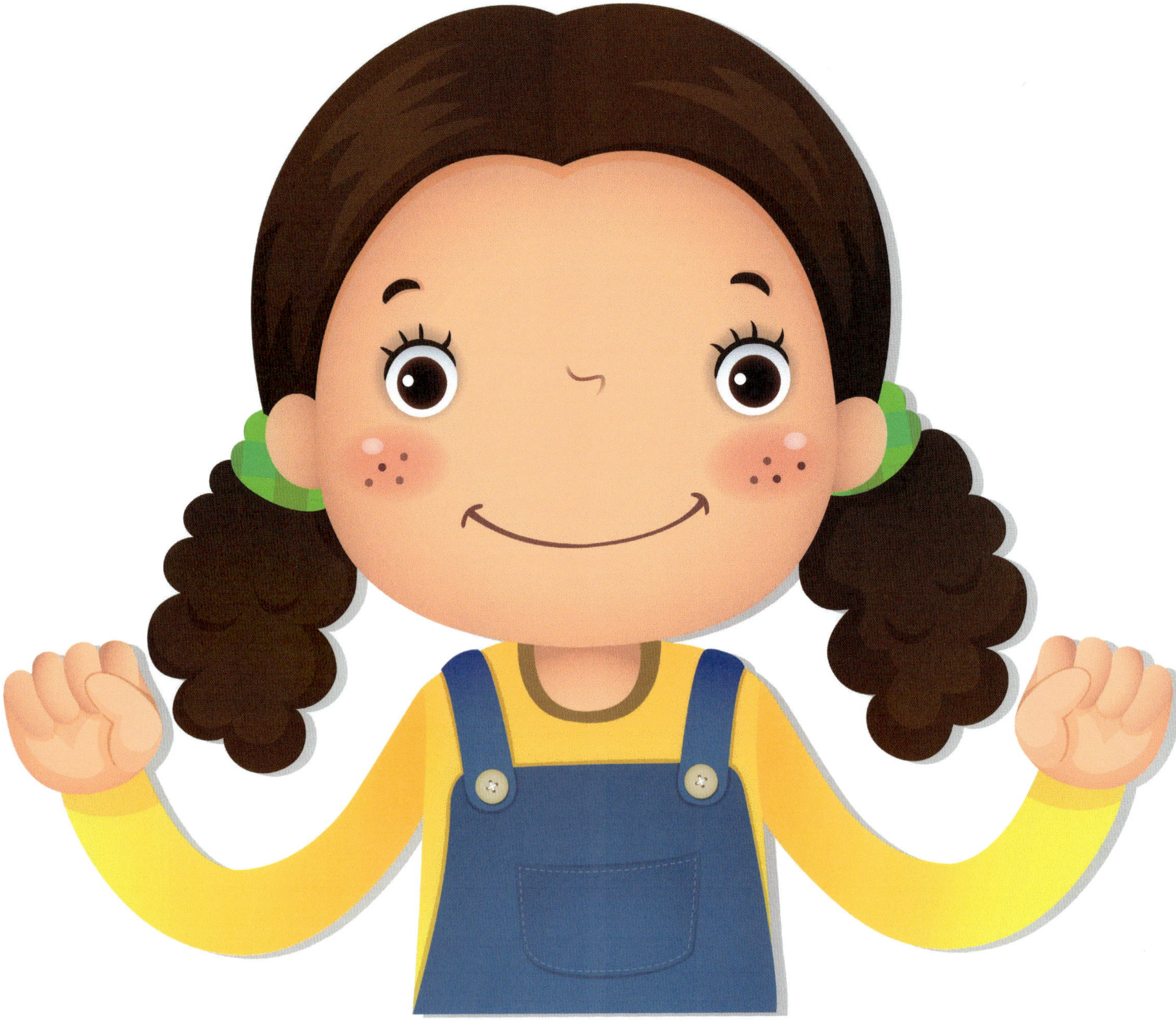

Opposites

happy

sad

confident

scared

Busy

lazy

Bored

excited

afraid

Brave

angry

happy

together / in love

apart / heart-Broken

friendly

Bully

sick

healthy

kind

mean

furious

calm

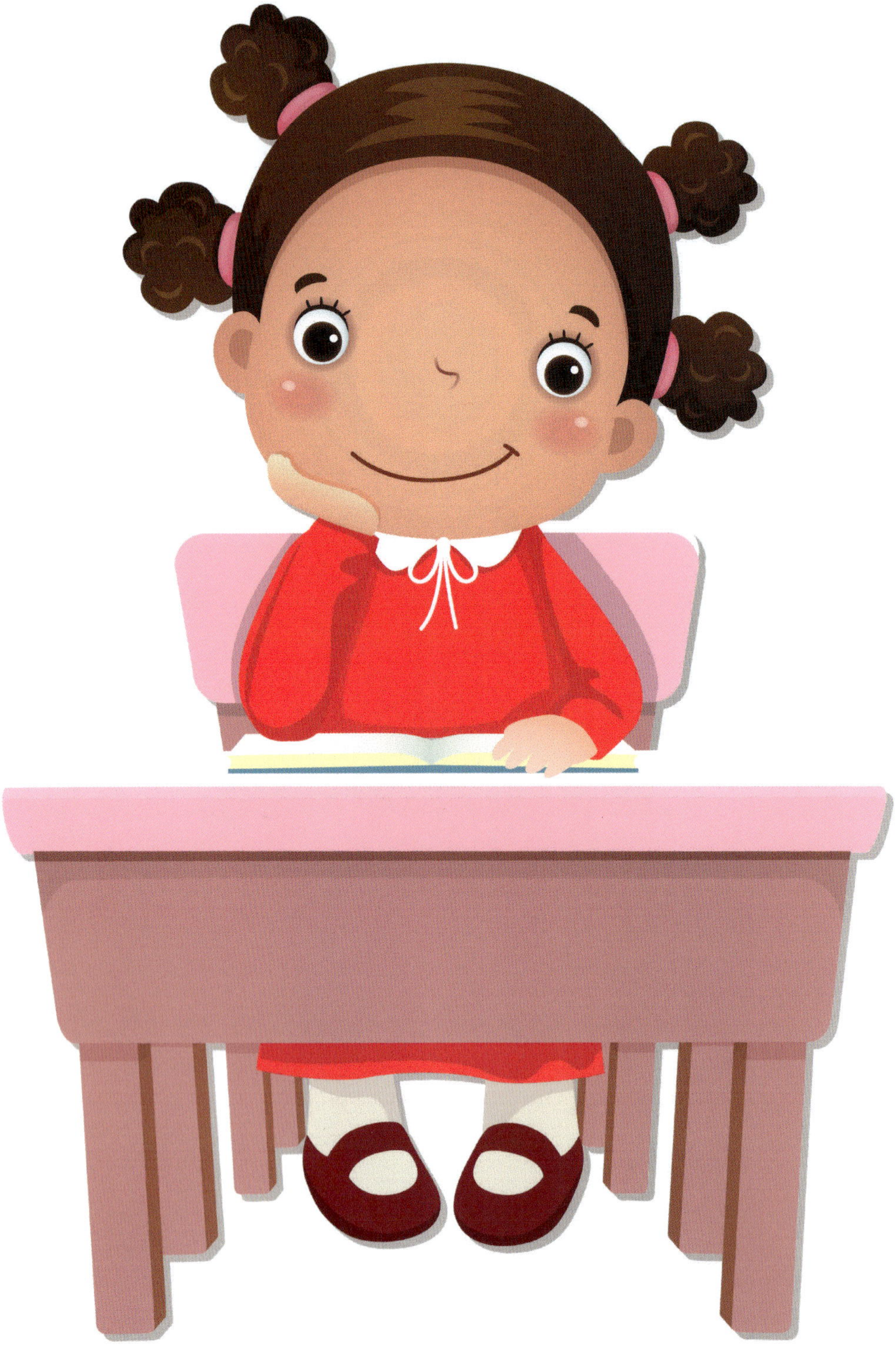

Let's identify some emotions with these quizzes!

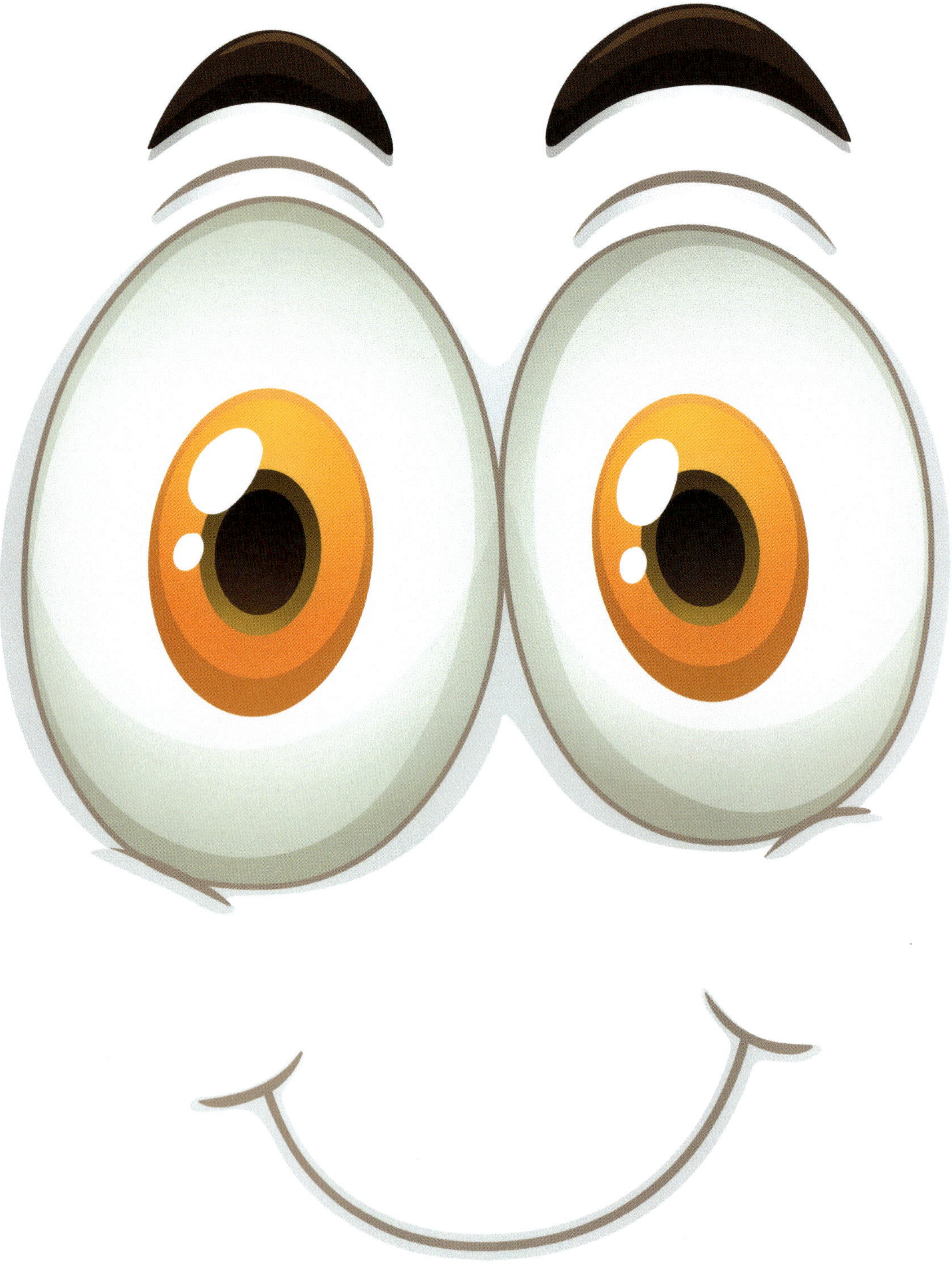

- [ ] confused
- [ ] happy
- [ ] angry
- [ ] afraid

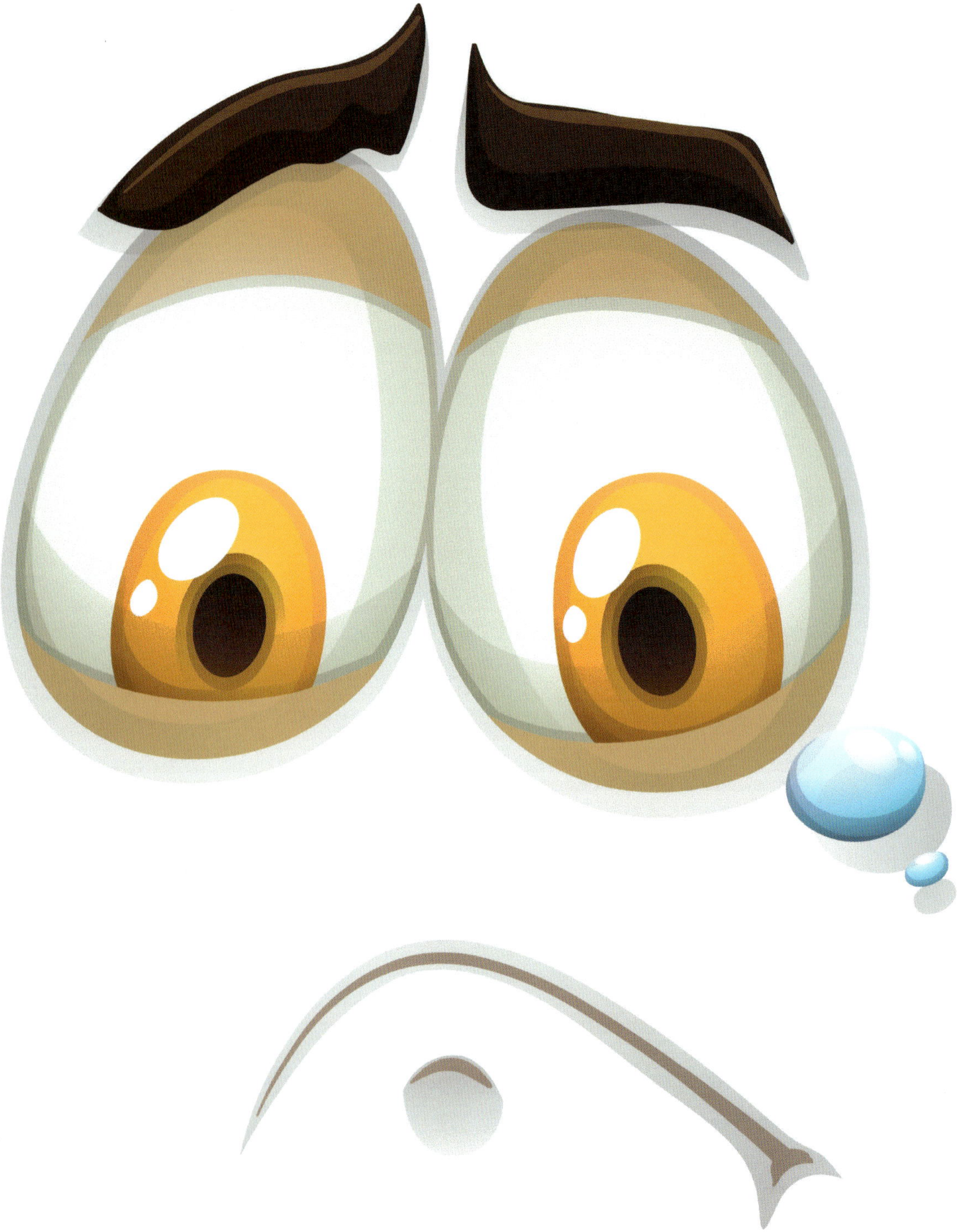

- [ ] cheeky
- [ ] suspicious
- [ ] sad
- [ ] glad

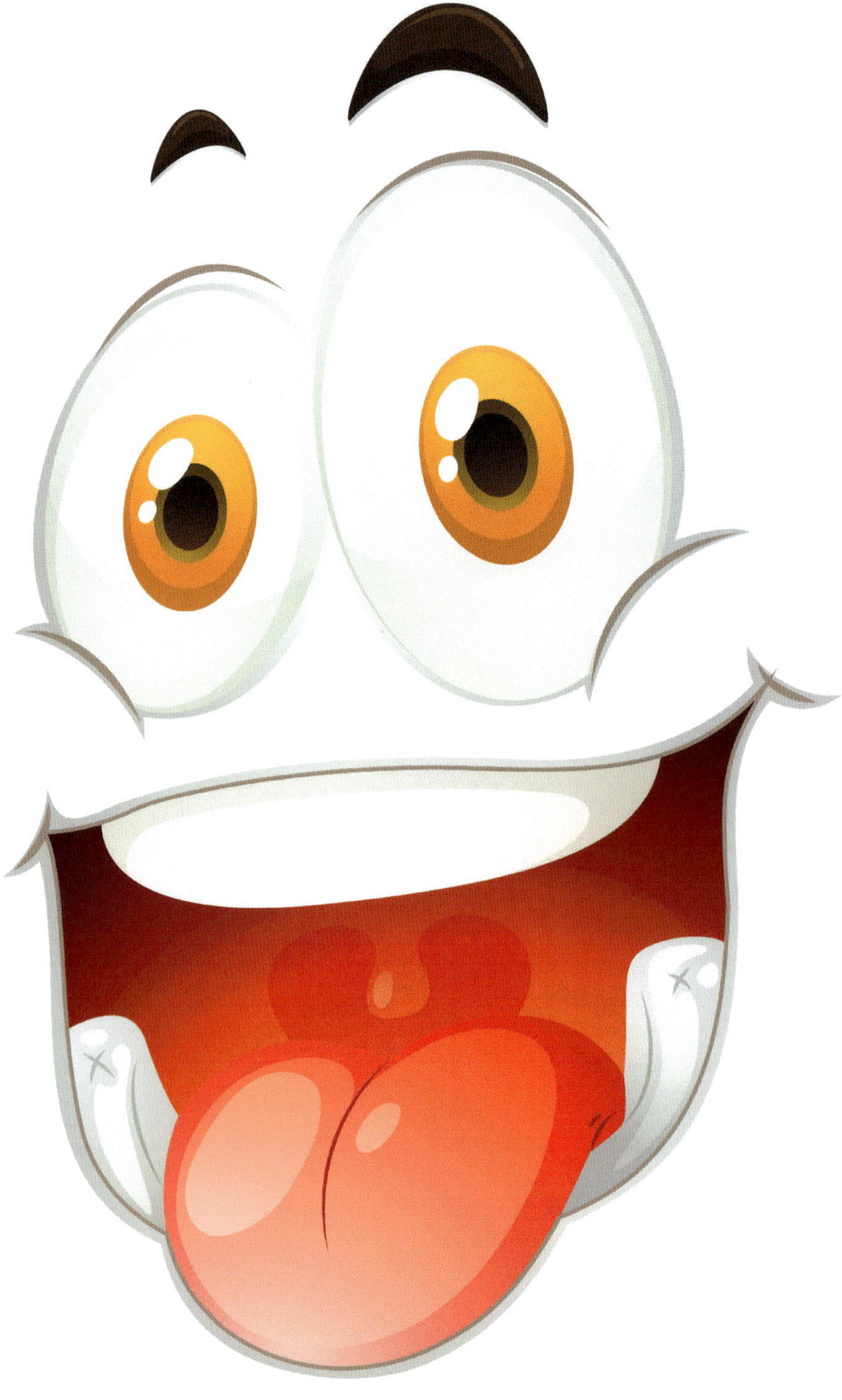

☐ excited

☐ bored

☐ sleepy

☐ mean

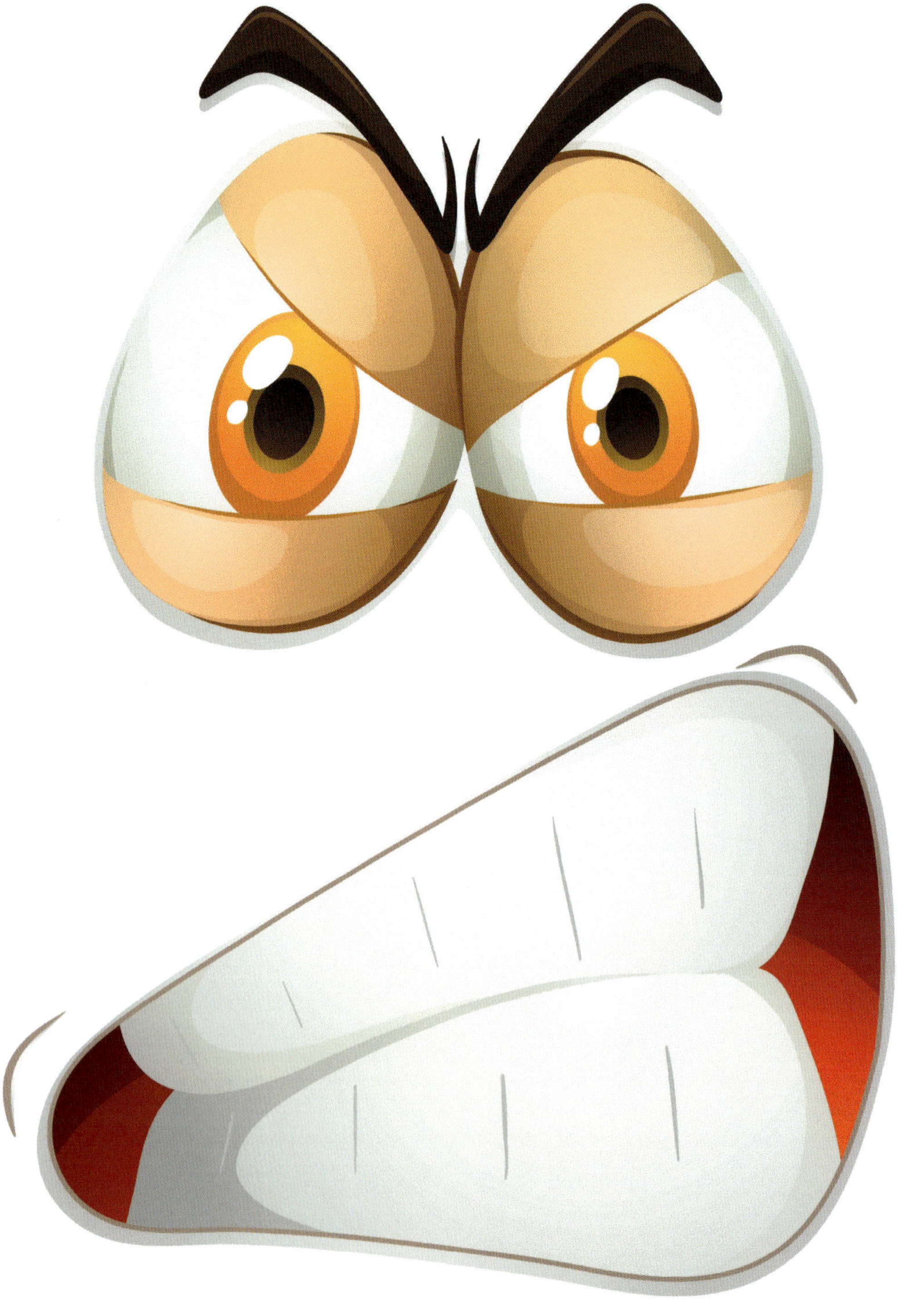

- [ ] exhausted

- [ ] furious

- [ ] surprised

- [ ] thoughtful

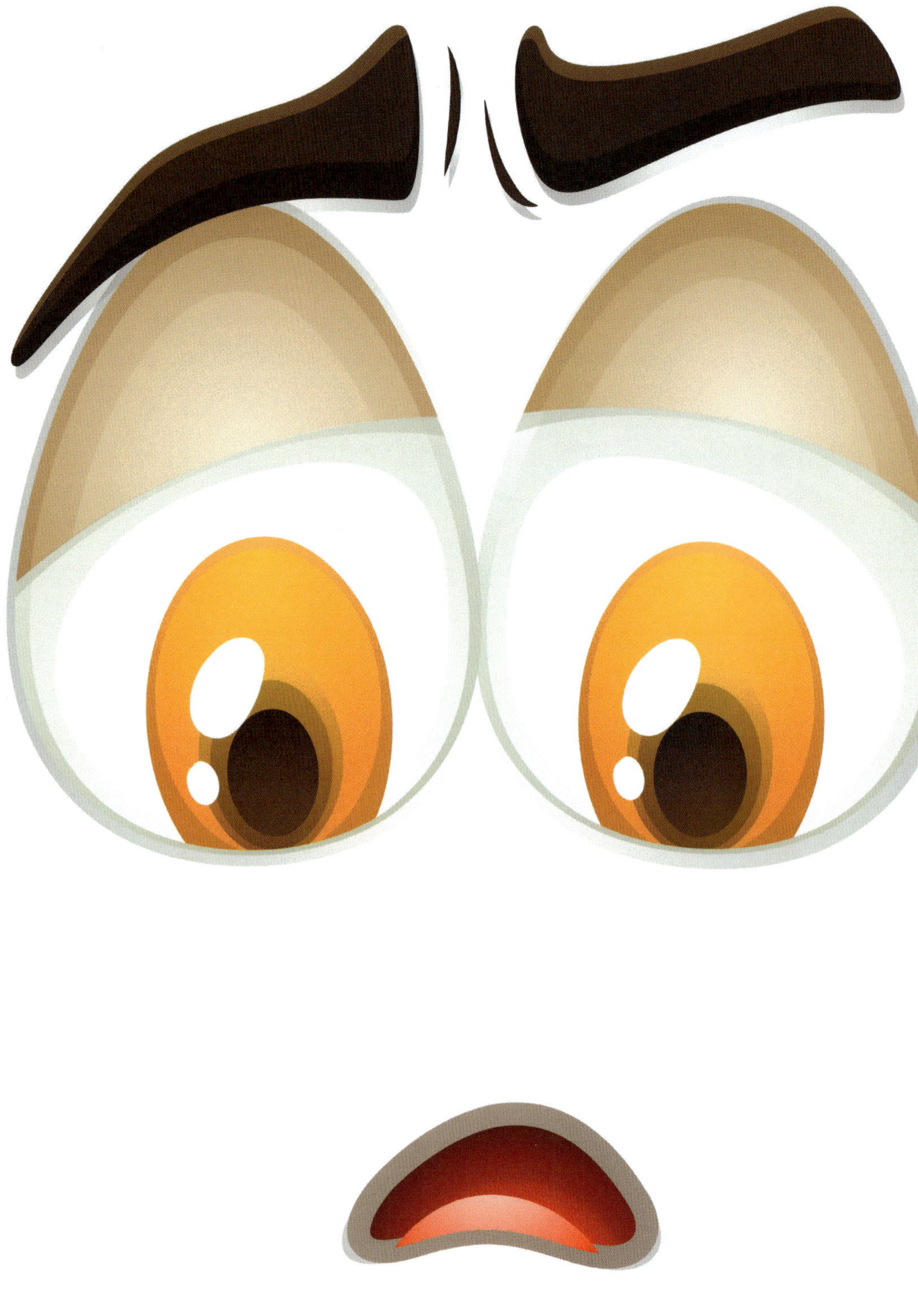

- [ ] happy

- [ ] calm

- [ ] friendly

- [ ] disappointed

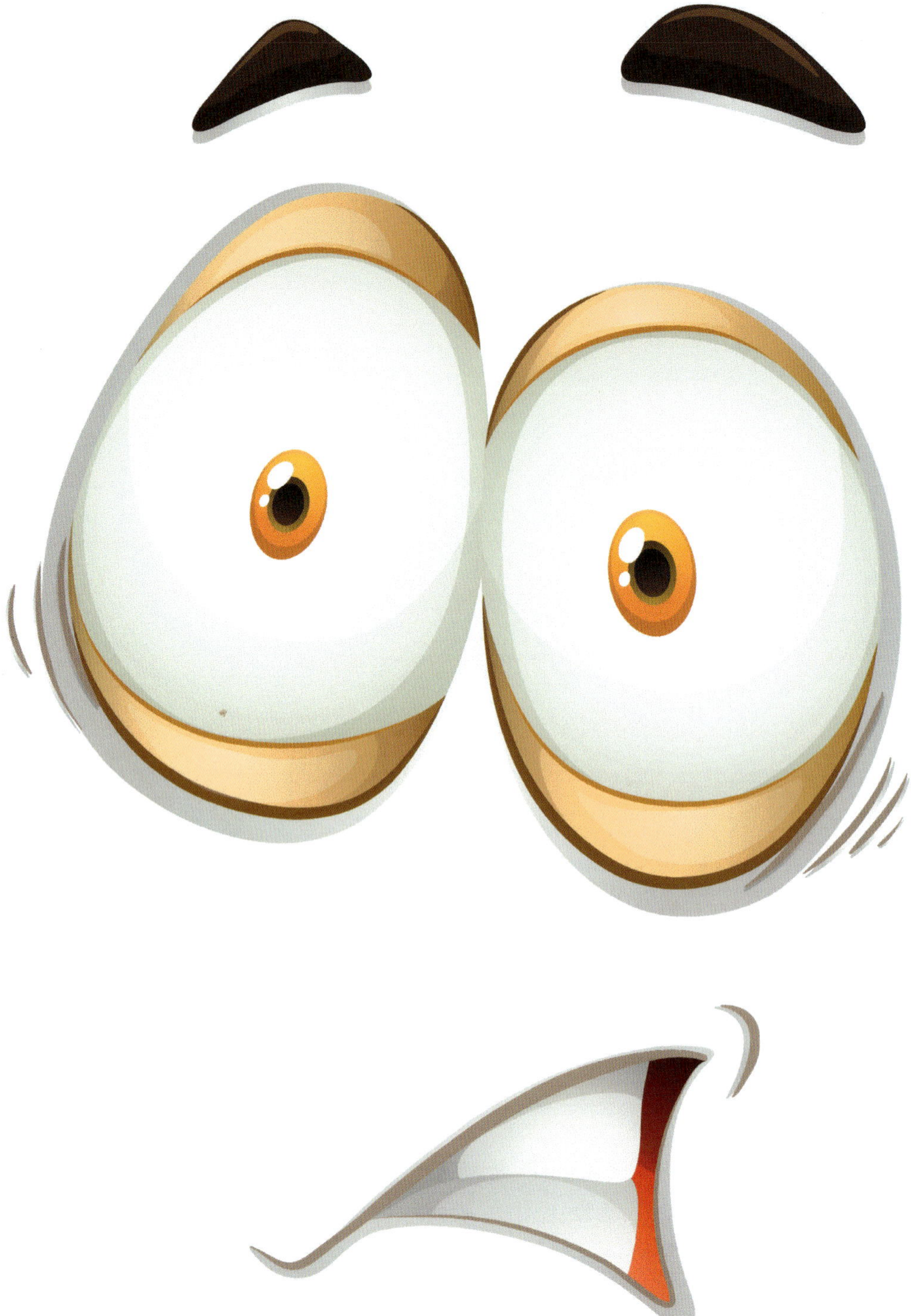

- [ ] crying
- [ ] mad
- [ ] shocked
- [ ] pleased

answers

happy	 furious
 sad	 disappointed
 excited	 shocked

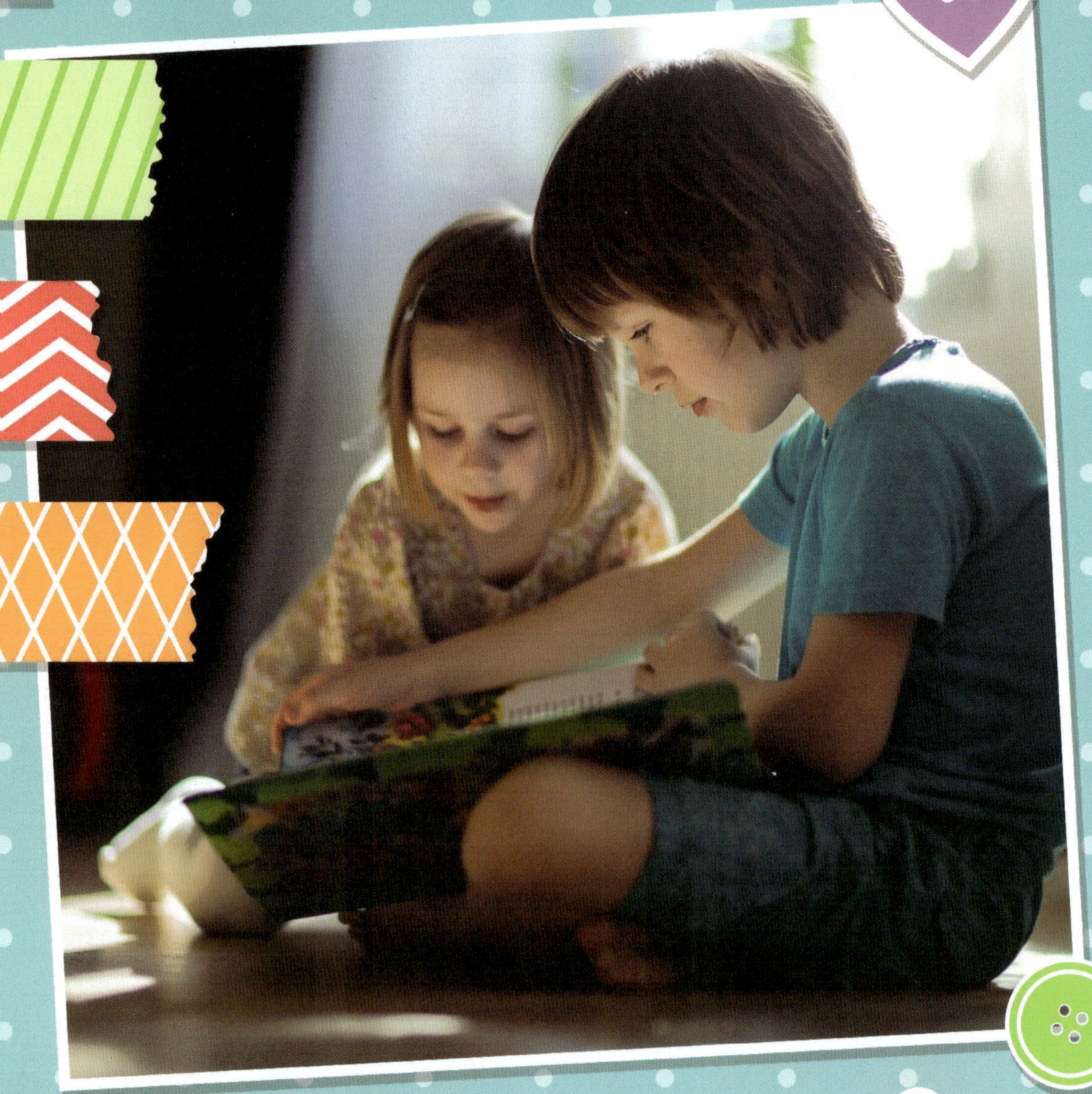

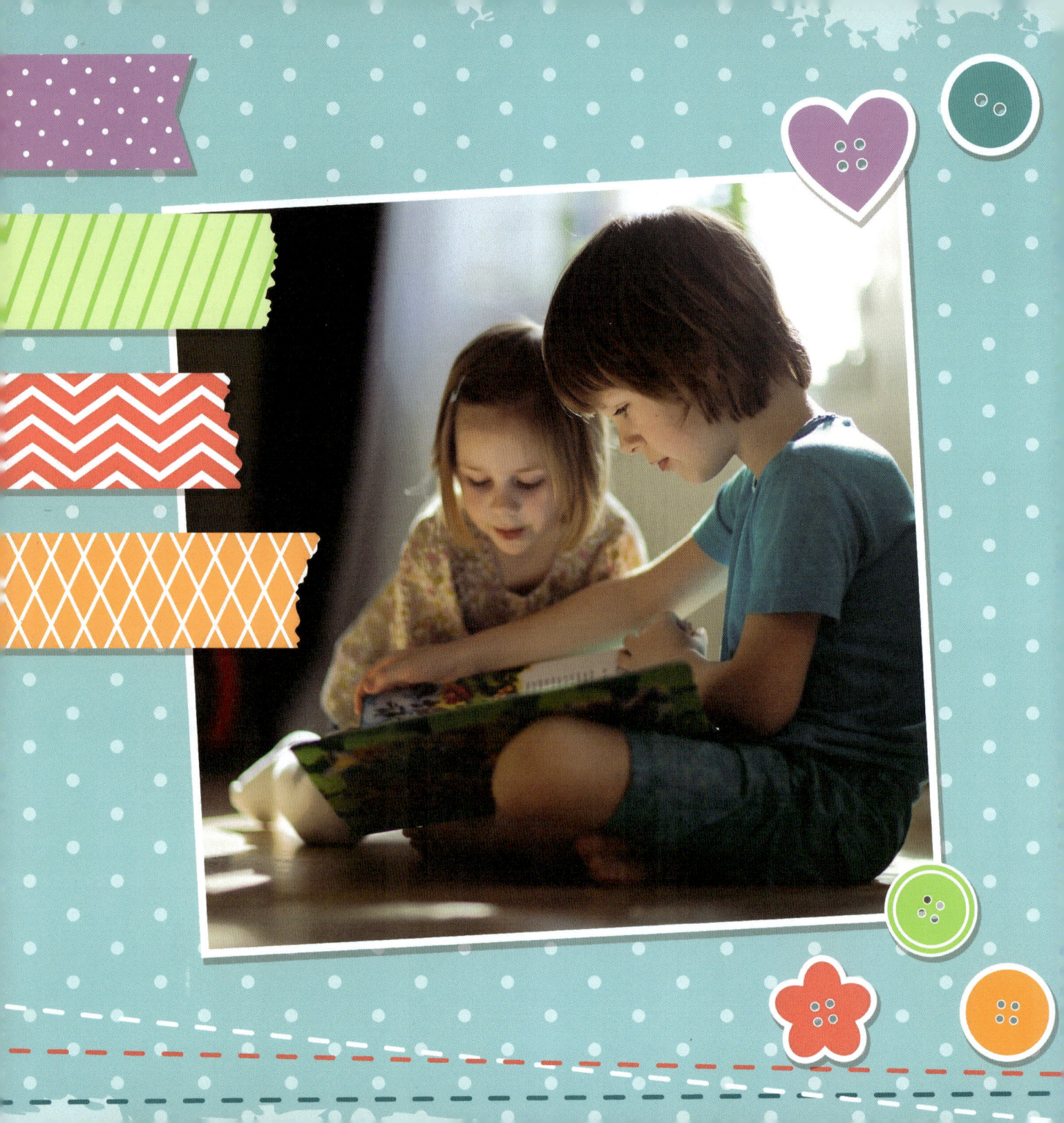

Visit

BABY PROFESSOR
EDUCATION KIDS

www.BabyProfessorBooks.com

to download Free Baby Professor eBooks and view our catalog of new and exciting Children's Books

Printed in Great Britain
by Amazon